Service 123, from Clacton to Ipswich, was jointly operated by Eastern National and Eastern Counties. On 5 February 1983, Eastern National 1769 (MAR 791P), new in 1976, has arrived at Mistley from Clacton. She will return to Clacton after connecting with Eastern Counties LN539 (HVF 539L), new in 1972, which has arrived from Ipswich. LN539 has turned round at Rigby Avenue, and will return to Ipswich.

New to Bristol Omnibus Company in January 1979, Badgerline TTC 537T is seen in Bath on 15 August 1992, boarding passengers for service 176 to Shepton Mallet.

West's of Woodford Green obtained the Essex County Council contract for service 201 from Buckhurst Hill to Ongar in 1986. On 24 May 1987, HVF 544L, new to Eastern Counties as LN544 in 1973, was seen in Ongar. In the background an Eastern National Leyland National has lost its National Bus Company emblems following privatisation in December 1986.

Eastern Counties LN577 (PVF 357R) was transferred to Ipswich Depot in 1986. In this view taken the same year, she is seen in Kesgrave in the hands of the Woodbridge out-station, working service 83 back into Ipswich from Melton.

11.3 metres long and with fifty-two seats, DPW 781T was new to Eastern Counties in 1979 with fleet number LN781. In 1981 she was fitted with a Gardner 6HLX engine and a front radiator, and was reclassified LG781. Later she gained a Leyland National 2 front. In this form LG781 was parked on layover at King's Lynn bus station on 10 April 1993. There is a Gardner engine badge below the Leyland badge on the front radiator grille.

London Transport's KJD 538P was captured on a hot summer's day at Golders Green in 1989. New in August 1976, by now she was part of the London Northern company, created in preparation for privatisation.

11.3 metres long and with fifty-two seats, Eastern Counties LN765 (XNG 765S) was new in 1978. She was rebuilt by East Lancashire as a National Greenway, and was reclassified LG765 because she received a Gardner 6HLXB engine. LG765 was at Surrey Street bus station in Norwich on 7 October 1995, waiting to depart to Sheringham and Cromer on the north Norfolk coast.

Fancy having your hair cut in a Leyland National? Well back in 2003 you could. NFM 853M was new to Crosville as ENL853 and was photographed at South Mimms in 2003.

Badgerline 3602 (A202 YWP) in the snow at Foundation Street Depot in Ipswich on 27 December 1996. This Leyland National 2, with a Gardner 6HLXCT engine and forty-seven semi-coach seats, was new to Midland Red West in 1984 and transferred to Badgerline in 1989. She was then transferred within FirstBus Group to Eastern Counties.

New to Eastern National in April 1978 as YEV 313S, Beestons MIL 4682 was photographed in 2000 in Sudbury, Suffolk, on local service 320 to Great Cornard. She was sold by Eastern National in September 1994 to Bristol Coach & Bus, and then to Volvo, Warwick, where a Volvo engine was fitted in August 1995. She then moved to Yeates, Loughborough, in August 1996, and then to Beeston, Hadleigh, in December 1996, where she was re-registered to MIL 4682.

Leyland National 2 A202 YWP is seen again, this time in Colchester bus station on 29 March 1997, waiting to return to Ipswich on service 92. Now numbered 642 in the Eastern Counties fleet, the semi-coach seats had been removed and replaced by bus seats. 642 was withdrawn from service in 2001.

Waiting for time at the foot of Bristol Hill in Shotley in 1984 is Eastern Counties LN764 (XNG 764S). The bus would turn around at the foot of the hill and return to Ipswich. In this view, she is in the care of the Woodbridge out-station.

Cambus 214 (PVF 365R) in Queensgate bus station at Peterborough on 5 June 1985. 11.3 metres long and with fifty-two seats, PVF 365R was new to Eastern Counties in 1976 with fleet number LN565. When Eastern Counties was split up in 1984, she became part of the Cambus fleet covering the western area of Eastern Counties.

Luton & District EPD 521V is seen in Watford on 11 March 1993. With B41F seating, this bus was new to London Country back in October 1979.

In February 1992, Cambus purchased Miller Coaches of Foxton, who had been running bus services in Cambridge in competition with Cambus. Then Cambus used the Millerbus name for certain services, including the Cambridge Park & Ride services. Cambus 304 (PEX 620W) was in Emmanual Street, Cambridge, on 1 July 1992 when seen. This Leyland National 2 was new to Eastern Counties in 1981 with fleet number LN620. She was 11.6 metres long, had forty-nine seats and a Leyland engine.

Having been new to Trent in December 1979, Leyland National FRA 534V was working for Bowers Coaches when photographed at Showbus, Duxford, in 2001.

Eastern National 1761 (MAR 783P) is seen arriving at Harwich bus station in April 1979 on a local service from Parkeston Quay. 1761 was a standard 11.3-metre-long Leyland National, and was new in 1976 with forty-nine seats. Under Badgerline ownership, Eastern National was split in to two in 1990, and 1761 became part of the Thamesway fleet serving south Essex. 1761 was withdrawn in 1992 and scrapped.

Although late in buying Leyland Nationals, London Transport did eventually take over 500 of the type, though only sixty-nine were of the later National 2 variety. In 1990, GUW 452W, new in April 1981, loads at London Bridge station on one of the Red Arrow services.

Thameswary 1853 (YEV 311S) in Chelmsford bus station on 10 April 1995, waiting to work home to Southend. A standard Leyland National, 11.3 metres long and with forty-nine seats, she was new to Eastern National in 1978. She was withdrawn in November 1995 and was transferred to South Wales Transport for spares.

New to Red & White in February 1977 with DP48F bodywork, Leyland National NWO 454R was still working for that company when photographed at Chepstow on 19 May 1992.

Eastern National 1938 (STW 19W) climbs North Hill in Colchester on 5 April 1994. One of a batch of Leyland National 2s purchased in 1980, she is 11.6 metres long, with Leyland engine and forty-nine seats. 1938 was transferred in October 1994 to Rider (York), another company in the Badgerline Group.

Leaving the bus station in Slough on 22 May 1993 is NRD 136M, working for The Bee Line. By now she was approaching twenty years old, having been new to Alder Valley back in September 1973.

11.3 metres long and with fifty seats, WNO 562L was new to Eastern National in 1973 with fleet number 1713. After fifteen years' service with Eastern National she was sold to East Midland, becoming 534 in that fleet. East Midland had opened a depot at Tintwistle near Glossop to operate services in Greater Manchester. Thus, 534 was at East Didsbury in south Manchester when seen on 17 June 1989.

In use when required by Konectbus back in 2009 was UFX 852S, seen here at Showbus, Duxford, that same year. This bus had been new to Hants & Dorset in November 1977, and is still in use today on school services in Norfolk with Lynx (*see page 93*). (Photograph: Tim Moore).

A standard 11.3-metre-long Leyland National with forty-nine seats, TJN 505R was new to Eastern National in 1977 with fleet number 1806. She was sold in 1994 but avoided being scrapped; instead, she was rebuilt by East Lancashire as a National Greenway and was fitted with a Gardner 6HLXB engine. She saw further service with Blackburn Borough Transport with fleet number 428, and is seen in Blackburn bus station on 5 July 1995.

New to the Bristol Omnibus Company in June 1976, Badgerline's KHT 123P passes through Radstock on 18 May 1992, bound for Bristol on service 178.

Colchester Borough Transport did not purchase any new Leyland Nationals, but under British Bus ownership from 1993 some Leyland National 2s were transferred in from Midland Fox. 9 (BVP 809V) is seen in Colchester bus station on 4 October 1995. She was new to Midland Red in 1980 with fleet number 809 and was 11.6 metres long with a Leyland engine and forty-nine seats.

New in February 1979 to Eastern Counties, Leyland National LN783 (DPW 783T) carried this advertising livery for the Army back in 1980. Not a regular Ipswich-based vehicle, she is however seen here in Ipswich during her brief visit here.

Colchester Borough Transport 351 (NIW 6511) entering Colchester bus station on 7 May 1997. This bus, a standard 11.3-metre-long Leyland National with forty-nine seats, was new as Hants & Dorset 3650 (LPR 938P) in 1976. Rebuilt as a National Greenway in 1993 and fitted with a Gardner engine, she was transferred from London & Country to Colchester in 1996.

Competition was rife in the St Albans area of Hertfordshire back in the early nineties, as seen here in this view of BusyBus TPD 192M and Sovereign WJN 558S on 28 May 1992. The BusyBus Leyland National had been new to London Country in January 1974, while the one working for Sovereign had been new to Eastern National in January 1978.

London Country Bus Services' first Leyland Nationals were 11.3 metres long with dual doorways (type 1151/2R/0402). LN7 (NPD 107L) was new in 1973 and is seen in later life after conversion to an information bus, at Stevenage bus garage on 17 May 1980.

Another rear view here. Eastern National were a huge supporter of the Leyland National, and here we see YEV 308S standing Colchester in 2000. This bus was new in April 1978.

London Country LNC38 (NPD 138L) was new in 1973, painted in a half green half white livery for use on Green Line coach services, even though she was fitted with bus seats. Here, NPD 138L was seen in later life with Yorkshire Terrier in Sheffield city centre on 22 July 1989.

Ribble's 786 (CBV 786S) was new in March 1978 and is seen here at Pilling on 1 March 1985. (Photograph: Peter Horrex collection).

Later London Country Leyland Nationals for Green Line services were 10.3 metres long with thirty-nine semi-coach seats. They were replaced on Green Line services by proper coaches from 1977 onwards and were then used on bus services, retaining the semi-coach seats. However, in this view of SNB160 (HPF 310N) in St Albans on 16 May 1981, she is working on Green Line service 707 from Luton Airport to London Victoria.

New to Eastern Counties in April 1981 was PEX 620W. In this 1996 view she was working for Stagecoach Cambus, but wearing the Millerbus variation of the Cambus livery when seen in Cambridge.

Leyland developed a simpler and cheaper Leyland National, the series B, available only in 10.3-metre length as type 10351B/1R, with a conventional heating system that dispensed with the heating and ventilation pod on the rear roof. London Country built up a large fleet, and shown here at West Croydon bus station on 25 May 1981 is SNB520 (EPD 520V). Seating capacity was for forty-one, with a luggage pen located over the front nearside wheel arch.

I've never been a lover of the East Lancs conversion of the National to the Greenway, but they do need to be included in this book. Seen working for Arriva Colchester in 2000 is NIW 6509, which was new in July 1977 to Hants & Dorset as TEL 491R.

TPD 178M was new to London Country in 1973 as fleet number SNB78. She was 10.3 metres long with forty-one seats and a luggage pen. When London Country was split up prior to deregulation and privatisation, SNB78 moved to London Country North East. Later, she saw further service with Reg's Coaches of Hertford, then with Blue Triangle Buses, as seen here in Romford on 29 March 1991.

In the summer of 2000, Neaves were operating ex-London Transport Leyland National THX 139S, photographed here passing through the bus station in Great Yarmouth. She was new in April 1978.

London Country Bus Services was split in to four operating companies prior to deregulation and privatisation, and later London Country North East was split further into County and Sovereign. Sovereign Buses SNB193 (LPB 193P) is seen in Stevenage bus station on 28 June 1989 while working a local service. She was new to London Country in 1976 as SNC193 with thirty-nine semi-coach seats.

In November 1972, Ribble purchased Leyland National PTF 729L, seen here working for Pride of the Road in 1991. (Photograph: Peter Horrex collection).

10.3 metres long and with forty-one seats and a luggage pen, NPK 241R was new to London Country in 1976 with fleet number SNB241. She was acquired by Southend Transport in 1990 from London Country Bus (South West) and is seen here in Southend central bus station on 10 April 1995.

Eastern Counties LN782 (DPW 782T) is seen in Dennington, Suffolk, on a winter's day in 1985. The main 273 service ran between Ipswich and Stradbroke, with shorter workings outward bound to Framlingham or Dennington. In the care of the Woodbridge out-station this bus is about to return home.

London Transport bought batches of 10.3-metre-long, dual-doorway, thirty-six-seat Leyland Nationals, mainly to replace AEC Merlins and Swifts. LS347 (AYR 347T) was allocated to Harrow Weald garage when photographed in Harrow on 27 March 1981.

South Wales Transport (SWT) Leyland National TWN 801S was purchased new by the company in June 1978. In this view she is seen leaving the bus station in Swansea on 21 May 1992.

London Transport LS222 (THX 222S) was new in 1978 and gained a special livery for Hillingdon local service 128. However, when seen at Hounslow bus station on 25 March 1989, LS222 was working on service 222 from Hounslow to Uxbridge.

Beestons of Hadleigh in Suffolk were operating this pair of Leyland Nationals when photographed in Sudbury back in 1995. Nearest the camera is RFS 586V, which, along with sister RFS 588V, was new to Scottish Omnibuses in April 1980.

Westlink was a low cost operation set up by London Regional Transport in 1986, to operate some bus services in south-west London. On 25 March 1989, Westlink LS314 (AYR 314T) was on layover at Hounslow bus station. She was a London Transport standard Leyland National, being 10.3 metres long with a dual-doorway layout and thirty-six seats.

Responding to competition from University Bus in the mid-1990s, Sovereign bus and coach formed Noddy Bus (after an employee who was already nicknamed Noddy). Noddy himself is seen here behind the wheel of BAZ 7378 in London Colney on 21 May 1994.

LS424 (BYW 424V) was new to London Transport in 1979 and was later transferred to Harrow Buses, a subsidiary of London Regional Transport. Seen here at Watford Junction station on 19 November 1990, it is working service 258 from South Harrow to Watford Junction – an example of a London Regional Transport service that operated beyond the Greater London Council boundary in to Hertfordshire.

Badgerline AAE 653V leaves Chepstow on 19 May 1992. This is one of many Leyland Nationals that moved to the Badgerline fleet when Bristol Omnibus was split, with this particular one being new in July 1980.

OJD 902R was new to London Transport in 1977 with fleet number LS102. After service in London, OJD 902R operated for Mybus, one of the many independent operators in Greater Manchester in the years after bus deregulation. Mybus were based at Hadfield, near Glossop, and operated local bus services from 1991 to 1994. On 11 August 1992, OJD 902R was photographed in Stockport bus station.

Leyland National RRM 148M was built as a demonstration vehicle in October 1973. Different to the standard National, this one was built with a completely flat floor and was marketed as Suburban Express. This bus remained unique and was eventually sold to Suffolk County Council, and then on to Woottens. The bus is currently preserved, and is seen here at Showbus, Duxford, in 2001.

For Red Arrow services, London Transport bought the Leyland National 2 in 1981. They were 10.6-metre-long, dual-doorway buses with twenty-four seats and space for forty-eight standees. After privatisation of the London bus companies, London General LS450 (GUW 450W) was at London Victoria station on 6 May 1991.

Another ex-Eastern National Leyland National in the Sovereign bus and coach fleet was WJN 558S, seen here at St Albans City station on 28 May 1992.

Alder Valley 151 (NRD 151M) is seen at Heathrow Airport on 2 July 1982. New in 1973, she was 11.3 metres long with forty-nine seats and a luggage pen. By the time of this image, many National Bus Company subsidiaries had undertaken the Market Analysis Project, which produced revised bus services and local identities. 151 has Wessexway local identity branding for services in the Alton area of Hampshire.

Eastern Counties closed their small out-station in Strabroke, Suffolk, in 1983. Shortly before the closure, Eastern Counties LN546 (HVF 546L) is seen parked outside the premises while operating a Saturday morning journey in the care of a Woodbridge out-station driver, as by now Stradbroke out-station only operated on weekdays.

Alder Valley 277 (TPE 170S) is seen leaving High Wycombe bus station on 27 November 1982, working an express service to Milton Keynes. New in 1978, she was 11.3 metres long with forty-five semi-coach seats plus a luggage pen. Many Leyland Nationals with this type of seating carried the National Bus Company's local coach livery; in this case, half red and half white.

Eastern Counties LN587 (WAH 587S) collects passengers in Felixstowe town centre in 1987, wearing that operator's deregulation livery, which seemed to suit the Leyland National, but did not look so good on double-deckers. This bus received the East Lancs Greenway conversion in December 1995 and still survives today in preservation.

Southdown 96 (AYJ 96T) was new in 1979 and was 11.3 metres long with a single doorway and fifty-two seats. She is seen here in Horsham town centre on 11 April 1981. Following service revisions in the Horsham area, Southdown had re-introduced the traditional gold fleet name on their buses operating there.

Red & White's NWO 475R departs Chepstow on 19 May 1992, heading for Danes on route 66. This Leyland National had been new to the company in October 1976.

After privatisation, Southdown re-introduced their traditional apple green and cream livery, as carried by 42 (RUF 42R) in Bexhill-on-Sea on 28 September 1989. 42 was new in 1977 as type 11351A/2R, and was 11.3 metres long with a dual-doorway layout and forty-four seats.

New to London Transport in May 1981, London Buses GUW 487W passes through New Oxford Street in 1991 when ten years old. She also received the East Lancs Greenway treatment a few years later.

Top Line 423 (BCD 823L) in Hastings on 30 June 1989. BCD 823L started life in 1973 with Southdown as fleet number 23, and was 11.3 metres long with a single doorway, forty-nine seats and a luggage pen. Top Line was a joint venture between Southdown and Eastbourne Buses, set up to compete with Hastings & District in the Hastings area. Hastings & District had been split off from Maidstone & District in 1983. Top Line was in operation from 1987 to 1989. Eventually, part of Southdown, Hastings & District and Eastbourne Buses all became part of the Stagecoach Group.

Ribble's 724 (UHG 724R), new in September 1976, is seen here passing through Burnley in 1985. (Photograph: Peter Horrex collection).

East Kent 1184 (EFN 184L), new in 1973, was an early 11.3-metre Leyland National with forty-nine seats and a luggage pen. Ten years later, on 20 May 1983, 1184 was in Maidstone, working home to Canterbury.

Back in the day when Showbus was still held each year at Woburn, West Midlands Travel OOX 830R is seen on 27 September 1992. Carrying DP45F bodywork, this Leyland National had been new to West Midlands PTE in July 1977.

When privatised, East Kent reverted to their traditional pre-National Bus Company livery of deep red and ivory. 1086 (NFN 86R), built in 1977, 11.3 metres long and fitted with forty-eight semi-coach seats, displays this livery in Canterbury bus station on 28 September 1990.

London Buses (Harrow Buses) Leyland National AYR 321T stands next to one of the new Metrobuses, E472 SON, in Harrow bus station in 1987. With a low seating capacity of just thirty-six, this bus was new in July 1979. Overhauled in April 1984, she remained in service in London until February 1991, before passing the following month to Pennine Blue via PVS (Carlton) and then moving on to CMT buses of Aintree, before being withdrawn and scrapped in 1997.

GKE 504L was an 11.3-metre-long Leyland National new to Maidstone & District in 1973 with fleet number 3504. She later became a driver training vehicle with East Kent, being renumbered P194, as seen at East Kent's Ashford Depot on 4 June 1985.

New to the Bristol Omnibus Company in April 1978, Badgerline's SAE 757S passes through Bath in 1991.

Maidstone & District 3518 (RKE 518M) is seen in the historic market town of Tenterden in Kent on 28 August 1986. 3518 carries the modified livery adopted with privatisation. The main colour is still National Bus Company green, but with a cream band, cream fleet name, no NBC symbols and dark green wheels and front bumper.

In March 1978, Alder Valley took delivery of Leyland National TPE 164S, which is seen here working for The Bee Line in Slough on 22 May 1993.

Maidstone & District 3521 (GKL 739N) was an 11.3-metre-long Leyland National new in 1974. 3521 was in Tunbridge Wells on 14 April 1990, displaying a later version of the privatised Maidstone & District livery with cream window surrounds.

Blazefield Buses was set up to respond to competition in the St Albans area that was affecting fellow Blazefield company Sovereign Bus & Coach. Here, Blazefield Buses VKE 564S loads at St Albans City station on 28 May 1992. She was new to Maidstone & District in September 1977.

Maidstone & District 3901 (SKN 901R) was one of a batch of 11.3-metre-long dual-purpose Leyland Nationals with forty-eight semi-coach seats delivered in 1977. 3901 was in Maidstone town centre on 27 September 1990, painted in Maidstone Park & Ride livery, but was on this occasion working service 5 to Hastings.

New in 1977 to London Transport as LS101, London Northern's OJD 901R passes through Camden Town in 1989. Receiving an overhaul in 1982, she remained in London until February 1990, subsequently working for Pride of the Road until 1995. She was acquired that same year by Fleet Jet of Hull, and was subsequently cut up on site.

11.3 metres long and fitted with forty-eight semi-coach seats, SKN 910R was new to Maidstone & District in 1977 with fleet number 3910. In 1983 the Hastings area of Maidstone & District was split into a separate company, Hastings & District. 3910 transferred to Hastings & District, renumbered 310, and is seen in Hastings on 28 August 1986.

One of a large number of Leyland Nationals in the Eastern National fleet, BNO 664T was new to the company in July 1978. She is seen here arriving at the bus station in Colchester in 1996.

11.3 metres long with forty-nine seats and a luggage pen, United Counties 559 (ERP 559T) was a new in 1979. She is seen in Kettering bus station on 18 August 1982. Later, 559 received United Counties' privatisation livery of dark green with orange and cream stripes. After life with United Counties she passed to Choice Travel in Walsall for further service.

Ribble 460 (NTC 640M), new in April 1974, is captured in Morecambe in May 1991.

United Counties Leyland National 2 581 (NRP 581V) is seen in Hitchin on 17 August 1982. New in 1980, she was 11.6 metres long, had a Leyland engine, forty-nine seats and a luggage pen. When United Counties was split up prior to deregulation and privatisation, 581 passed to Luton & District for further service.

Keighley & District UWY 65X, a Leyland National with B52F bodywork that was new to West Yorkshire in July 1981, is seen here in Keighley in May 1991.

Northampton Transport was a keen operator of Daimler buses, so Daimler Fleetline single-deckers were purchased for one-person operation. However, British Leyland stopped production of other makes of single-decker to boost sales of the Leyland National, so Northampton Transport bought twelve Leyland Nationals in 1974 and 1975. They had dual doorways and were 11.3 metres long, and one of them was 25 (PNH 25N), which is seen turning in to Greyfriars bus station in Northampton on 15 April 1982.

Another Leyland National in the Badgerline fleet that was new to the Bristol Omnibus Company (January 1979) is TTC 536T, seen here in Bath on 15 August 1992.

KDW 352P was a 11.3-metre-long Leyland National with semi-coach seats, new to Red & White in 1975 with fleet number ND675. Later she became part of the National Welsh fleet with fleet number ND4475. She was acquired by Lincolnshire Road Car in 1992 from Barnards of Kirton Lindsey. She is seen at Lincolnshire Road Car's Newark-on-Trent Depot on 12 October 1992.

In 1980 Eastern National received fifteen Leyland National 2 with Leyland engines, each of which was 11.6 metres long and had forty-nine seats. Allocated to Braintree, 1930 (MHJ 726V) was on layover in Braintree bus park on 3 August 1980, when seen. On the extreme right is the rear of sister Leyland National 2 1929 (MHJ 725V).

The National Bus Company's Market Analysis Project was used extensively by Midland Red to develop viable bus networks and one feature of the revised bus services was local identity branding. Midland Red 699 (TOF 699S) was new in 1978. 11.3 metres long and with forty-nine seats, she is seen in Wellington, Shropshire, in October 1980. She carries Tellus branding for bus services in the Telford area.

11.3 metres long and with forty-nine seats, Eastern National 1833 (VAR 899S) was new in 1977. When photographed at Colchester bus station on 23 May 1987, she carried an overall advert for Bates of Maldon while working home to Maldon Depot on service 119 from Clacton.

In preparation for deregulation and privatisation, many National Bus Company subsidiaries were split up. Midland Red was divided four ways: North, East, South, West. Midland Red North used the local identity branding instead of a fleet name. 651 (PUK 651R), seen at Tamworth on 7 June 1985, carries Mercian branding.

Eastern National 1920 (JHJ 146V) was new in 1979 and was 11.3 metres long with forty-nine seats. On 4 October 1986, 1920 was allocated to Harwich Depot, and she was seen while on layover outside the depot, fresh from a repaint into Eastern National's privatisation livery of dark green and yellow.

11.3 metres long and with forty-nine seats, Midland Reed North 704 (TOF 704S) was new in 1978. She is seen at Wellington Depot in Shropshire on 9 March 1990, having been repainted into a later livery. The Tellus local identity name had become part of the fleet name.

ORP 462M was new to United Counties in 1973, 11.3 metres long with fifty-two seats. Coastal Red acquired her in September 1987. On 6 February 1988, when seen, she was on layover in Colchester bus station, working service 105 from Walton-on-the-Naze, a service tendered by Essex County Council. Twenty-two days later Coastal Red was acquired by Eastern National and the Coastal Red buses were disposed of in May 1988.

After the split up of Midland Red, Midland Red East became Midland Fox and adopted a revised livery with a yellow front, as displayed by 3826 (EON 826V) in Leicester on 7 June 1985. This Leyland National 2 was 11.6 metres long, had a Leyland engine and forty-nine seats, and had been new to Midland Red in 1980. In 1994, when Midland Fox was under British Bus control, she moved from Midland Fox to Colchester Borough Transport for further service.

London Country Bus Services SNB372 (YPF 772T) was a 10.3-metre-long Leyland National with forty-one seats and was new in 1978. She was photographed in Stevenage on 17 May 1980. The large Stevenage Bus branding provides some contrast to the standard National Bus Company livery.

London Regional Transport commenced route tendering in 1985. The tendering process was designed to encourage operators both large and small to participate. Tellings Golden Miller Coaches used the TGM Buses fleet name, as seen here on their 3562 (NOE 562R) in Hounslow on 1 October 1991. At this time there was no requirement for overall red livery, but a London Transport Service notice was displayed. NOE 562R was new to Midland Red in 1976.

OKJ 514M was new to Maidstone & District in 1974, an 11.3-metre-long Leyland National with forty-nine bus seats. Later transferred to East Kent and renumbered from 3514 to 1514, on 4 June 1985 she was being prepared for an unusual working for a Leyland National – National Express service 025 to Gatwick Airport.

11.3 metres long and with seating capacity forty-nine, Western National 2804 (GFJ 668N) was new in 1975. She was photographed in Penzance on 3 October 1981, complete with Cornish Fairways branding to give a local identity to Western National's services in Cornwall.

Brighton Borough Transport 31 (XFG 31Y) was new in March 1983, so she was less than two months old when seen at Brighton Borough Transport's depot on 1 May 1983. XFG 31Y was a Leyland National 2 and was 11.6 metres long, powered by a Gardner 6HLXB engine and fitted with forty-nine semi-coach seats.

11.3 metres long and with fifty-two seats, VOD 601S was new to Western National in 1978 with fleet number 2861. The years after bus deregulation saw the gradual formation of large groups. Badgerline Holdings was formed in 1986, and in 1988 both Western National and Midland Red West were acquired. VOD 601S was transferred within Badgerline from Western National to Midland Red West. She gained fleet number 601 in the Midland Red West fleet and is seen at Redditch on 21 April 1990.

United Counties 450 (GBD 450L) is seen at Letchworth on 17 August 1982. She was United Counties' first Leyland National, new in 1973, and was 11.3 metres long with forty-nine seats. The brown fleet number plate with black edging denoted allocation to Hitchin Depot.

Chesterfield Borough Transport 25 (EKY 25V) was a 10.6-metre-long, Leyland-engined Leyland National 2 new in 1980 with forty-four seats. She is seen in Chesterfield town centre on 12 June 1984.

11.3 metres long and with fifty-two seats, East Midland 506 (GCY 745N) was new in 1974 to South Wales Transport. In later life she passed to East Midland, as seen here while working in Chesterfield on 27 March 1989.

Chesterfield Borough Transport 50 (B150 DHL) is seen in Chesterfield town centre on 27 March 1989. This 11.6-metre-long Leyland National 2 fitted with semi-coach seats was new in 1984 and was powered by a Gardner 6HLXCT engine. The option for a Gardner engine in the Leyland National had been requested by operators for a long time, but only became available during the production run of the Leyland National 2.

11.3 metres long and fitted with fifty bus seats, West Midlands Travel 1484 (TOE 484N), photographed in Solihull on 28 April 1990, was new in 1974. West Midlands Travel was established to take over the bus services of West Midlands Passenger Transport Executive after the deregulation of bus services in 1986, and later became part of the National Express Group.

Potteries Motor Traction (PMT) 306 (A306 JFA) is seen at Shrewsbury bus station on 15 June 1984, loading up to work home to Hanley in the Potteries. 306 was new in 1984 with forty-seven semi-coach seats. This Leyland National 2 was type NL116HLXCT/1R, denoting its 11.6-metre length, Gardner 6HLXCT engine, single door and right-hand drive.

In July 1978 South Wales took delivery of Leyland National TWN 802S. She was photographed in Neath on 21 May 1992 wearing the livery of the time for South Wales Transport.

Chase Coaches, based at Chasetown near Walsall, developed a network of local bus services after deregulation, mainly using second-hand Leyland Nationals. Chase Coaches had extensive workshop facilities to overhaul and refurbish Leyland Nationals. This was the scene in part of the workshops on 24 March 1994, with a rear view of two unidentified Leyland Nationals.

Another Leyland National that was new to London Transport was OJD 898R, which was new as LS98 in August 1977 with B36D bodywork. She is seen here, preserved, at Showbus, Duxford, in 1999.

10.3 metres long with a dual-doorway layout and thirty-six seats, AYR 330T started life as London Transport LS330 in 1979. Fifteen years later she has been overhauled and rebuilt to a single doorway forty-four-seat bus in Chase Coaches' workshops. She was photographed at Chase Coaches' depot on 24 March 1994.

London Country's SNB319 (UPB 319S) had been new in November 1977, and was still working for of the companies that evolved from the division of London Country following deregulation. By the time she was photographed at Waltham Cross in 1990, the operating name being used was Townlink.

Crosville ENL948 (LMB 948P) is seen at Northwich Depot on 3 January 1987. This image shows the high back semi-coach seats fitted to dual purpose Leyland Nationals. Crosville experimented with this dark green and orange livery around the period of deregulation and privatisation.

A picturesque scene here in 1980 as Eastern Counties LN598 (WVF 598S) heads out of Shottisham in Suffolk, bound for Bawdsey on route 286.

At first glance Crosville SNG367 (EMB 367S) looks like any other Leyland National in National Bus Company fleets. However, the Crosville fleet number SNG367 referred to single-deck, National, Gardner engine. SNG367 was one of a number of Leyland Nationals that Crosville re-engined with Gardner 6HLX engines taken from withdrawn Seddon Pennine RU single-deckers. She was photographed at Northwich Depot on 8 February 1986.

London Transports GUW 476W was delivered new to Aldenham Works in February 1981, but it was April before she entered service on the Red Arrow routes out of Victoria garage. In 1988 she was transferred to the depot at Waterloo to continue working on the Red Arrow services, and continued to do so after her East Lancs Greenway conversion in 1993, remaining here with the privatised company London General until her withdrawal in 2002. She ended her life with Multiplex UK as a shuttle bus for Wembley Stadium before being scrapped a few years later.

The English part of Crosville later adopted a dark green and cream livery, as seen here on SNG372 (GMB 372T) in Macclesfield bus station on 11 October 1986. SNG372 was new in 1978 and was 11.3 metres long with forty-nine seats. Originally fitted with a Leyland 510 engine, she had been repowered with a Gardner 6HLX engine from a withdrawn Seddon Pennine RU.

New to National Welsh in September 1978 was Leyland National WUH 167T, photographed here in Hereford on 22 May 1992 while working for Red & White.

Crosville Wales dual-purpose and Gardner-engined ENG967 (MLG 967P) is seen at Dolgellau Square on 2 May 1987. After bus deregulation on 26 October 1986, Gwynedd County Council specified that buses operating their supported services had to have red fronts and Bws Gwynedd branding, irrespective of operator. ENG967 shows the application of the red front to the Crosville Wales livery.

First Eastern Counties (Blue Bus) Leyland National PEX 617W had been new to Eastern Counties in November 1980 with B49F bodywork. In this 1998 view she is seen in the small bus station in Diss, Norfolk, prior to working back across the county to Great Yarmouth.

The South East Lancashire & North East Cheshire (SELNEC) Passenger Transport Executive took a small batch of Leyland Nationals for evaluation in 1972. They were among the first Leyland Nationals to be produced, with K suffix registrations. EX30 (TXJ 507K) has been preserved by the Greater Manchester Transport Museum and was seen outside the museum in Boyle Street on 31 October 2009. EX30 was 11.3 metres long, was of dual-doorway layout and had forty-four seats.

New to London Transport as LS503 in May 1981, GUW 503W spent her first year in service on the 501 route out of Walworth garage, before spending a couple of years in store before being overhauled at Aldenham in 1985. She became a driver training vehicle with First Centrewest in London in 1997, before continuing that role with First Eastern Counties from 1999, on and off until at least 2008. She is seen here in the bus station at Ipswich in 2000.

SELNEC PTE became Greater Manchester PTE following local government reorganisation. Further batches of Leyland Nationals were purchased, including Greater Manchester Transport 151 (JDB 103N), which was was 10.3 metres long. Seen at Glossop on 20 April 1985 while waiting to tackle the hills on the edge of the Derbyshire Peak District, she was working service 394 to Hazel Grove railway station near Stockport.

New to London Transport as LS447, GUW 447W was withdrawn in February 1994 and sold the following year to Parfitts of Rhymney Bridge, where she stayed for only eight months before being bought by The Shires, Luton, in August of that year. She is seen here in Luton in 1996, and she lasted three more years before being sold for scrap in 1999.

Wall's Coaches of Fallowfield in south Manchester expanded into local bus services after deregulation, mainly with double-deckers and a small number of Leyland Nationals. YSV 672, an 11.3-metre-long Leyland National new in 1977, was at Piccadilly Gardens bus station in Manchester on 9 April 1989 when photographed. She was originally Greater Manchester Transport 185 (RBU 185R).

Leyland National SBK 740S was new to Gosport & Fareham in July 1978 and was photographed here at Showbus, Duxford, in 2001.

In 1976 Greater Manchester PTE bought Lancashire United Transport, at that time the largest independent bus operator in the country, with a large number of its services operating within the PTE area. Batches of Leyland Nationals were ordered for the Lancashire United operations, which were gradually integrated with the PTE's own bus services. Seen at Spinning Jenny Lane bus station in Leigh on 19 June 1984 were 208 (NEN 954R), new in 1977, and 221 (PTD 667S), new in 1978. Both were 11.3 metres long with forty-nine seats.

London Transport's LS504 (GUW 504W), new in 1981, spent much of the 1980s either in store or being transferred between garages, spending just short periods of time in service. In the summer of 1991 she was upseated from B24D to B44F and transferred to Uxbridge garage, where she went to work on the 607 services, on which she was working when photographed at Uxbridge in 1993. She transferred from First Centrewest to First Eastern Counties in 2000, where she remained until 2006.

After deregulation, Greater Manchester Transport had surplus buses which were sold on for further service with other operators. 221 (PTD 667S) was operating with the independent Catch A Bus in the north-east when seen here in South Shields on 15 October 1988.

11.3 metres long and with forty-nine seats, KMA 406T was new to Crosville in 1979 with fleet number SNL406. She later received a Gardner 6HLX engine from a withdrawn Seddon Pennine RU, and was reclassified SNG406. In this form SNG406 is seen at Macclesfield bus station on 22 August 1986, prior to working service E8 to Stockport.

11.3 metres long and with fifty-two seats, RTC 645L was the first Leyland National that Widnes Corporation Transport purchased in 1972. Local government reorganisation saw Widnes become Halton, so here we see Halton Transport 1 (RTC 645L) in Widnes on 14 June 1984. RTC 645L was withdrawn in 1992 and was preserved at the North West Museum of Road Transport in St Helens.

Citibus was an independent operator that built up a network of local bus services in the years after deregulation, mainly in north Manchester. On 11 August 1992, Citibus FWA 476V was photographed at Ashton-under-Lyne bus station. This Leyland National 2 was new to South Yorkshire Passenger Transport Executive in 1980 and was 10.6 metres long with forty-four seats.

Halton Transport 28 (CKC 928X) is seen in Widnes on 14 June 1984, heading for Runcorn Shopping City. She was new in 1982 and was 11.6 metres long with fifty-two seats. She later saw service with Devaway of Chester and Arriva Wales.

11.3 metres long and with forty-nine seats, MBO 23P was new to Taff-Ely Borough Council in South Wales in 1976. She later saw service with the independent Yorkshire Terrier, as seen here in Sheffield city centre on 22 July 1989.

Yorkshire Woollen District 128 (HED 205V) is seen outside Huddersfield bus station on 26 April 1991. A Leyland National 2 with a Leyland engine, 11.6 metres long and with fifty-two seats, HED 205V was new to Halton Transport in 1980.

After Badgerline Holdings merged with Grampian Regional Transport Group in 1995 to form First Bus, the Rider (York) operations in York became First York. Before the adoption of corporate liveries, First York had a green livery with black window surrounds. This is shown on First York 1345 (PNW 598W), which was photographed in York on 17 June 2000. 11.6 metres long and with fifty-two seats, this Leyland National 2 was new to West Yorkshire Road Car Company in 1980.

Prior to deregulation and privatisation, Crosville had its Welsh operations transferred to a new company, Crosville Wales. 10.3 metres long and having forty-four seats, SNL658 (GMB 658T) was a Leyland National series B and was new to Crosville in 1978. On 25 April 1987, SNL658 was working for Crosville Wales, at Denbigh in Clwyd.

Three months after deregulation, the Bee Line Buzz Company launched high-frequency minibus services in Greater Manchester. Greater Manchester Buses responded with their Little Gem minibus services. This competition could not last. In September 1989 Drawlane Group bought the Bee Line Buzz Company, and over the next few years many of the minibuses were replaced by full size buses. One of these was 260 (NOE 558R), which is seen at Oldham (Mumps) on 19 February 1994. NOE 558R had transferred from Midland Red North and, 11.3 metres long with forty-nine seats, was originally new to Midland Red in 1976.

Merseyside Transport was the operating division of Merseyside Passenger Transport Executive. New in 1978, and 11.3 metres long with forty-nine seats, Merseyside Transport 6063 (RKA 869T) pulls out of St Helens bus station on 11 January 1986 with a good load of passengers.

In the summer of 1978 Eastern Counties took delivery of LN767 (XNG 767S), which is seen here in 1990 at Bawdsey while in the care of a driver from the Woodbridge out-station. Note the Leyland National parked in the churchyard, which was the parking area for the Bawdsey out-station.

Merseyside Transport Ltd (MTL) was the privatised Merseyside PTE operating company and ran competitive services in Greater Manchester. A new livery and local fleet names were introduced. MTL Manchester 5211 (AKY 611T) was a series B Leyland National with forty-four seats and was new to East Midland in 1979. She is seen in Princess Street in Manchester city centre on 26 March 1994.

Rosemary Coaches were by now part of the Eastern Counties fleet. New in November 1977, LN594 (WAH 594S) was being stripped for spare parts at King's Lynn Depot when seen on 6 April 1996. (Photograph: Tim Moore).

11.6 metres long with a Leyland engine and forty-nine seats, MTL Southport 6133 (VBG 133V) was a Leyland National 2 new in 1980 to Merseyside Transport. She is seen in Lord Street, Southport, on 12 August 1995. Southport Corporation Transport had become part of Merseyside Passenger Transport Executive following local government reorganisation in 1974.

New in September 1979 to London Transport as LS368, BYW 368V worked from a variety of London bus garages before finding herself being painted into this Kingfisher livery in 1989. She survived until the end of 1990, when she was withdrawn. Here she is seen in Kingston-upon-Thames in 1989 while working service 71 to Richmond.

Barrow Corporation Transport had a long history of buying Leyland buses, so it was not surprising to find Leyland Nationals in this fleet. 11.3 metres long and with forty-nine seats, 11 (NEO 829R) was new in 1977. She is seen in Barrow-in-Furness on 11 June 1984. As a result of the 1985 Transport Act, Barrow Corporation Transport became Barrow Borough Transport. Deregulation in 1986 brought competitive services from Stagecoach. Barrow Borough Transport ceased trading in 1989, and this bus passed to Stagecoach.

Passing through Watford on 11 March 1993 is Luton & District's UPB 328S, a Leyland National with B41F bodywork that was new in November 1977 to London Country.

11.6 metres long and with forty-nine seats, Barrow Corporation Transport 22 (CEO 722W) was a Leyland National 2 new in 1980. She is seen in Barrow-in-Furness on 11 June 1984. Barrow Borough Transport, as successor to Barrow Corporation Transport, ceased trading in 1989, and this bus passed to Stagecoach.

Showbus at Woburn in 1992 is the location for this photograph of East Lancs-bodied Greenway JCK 852W. Originally new to Ribble in September 1981 with B44F bodywork, she was by now working for London & Country, and the seating capacity had been downgraded to B41F.

Burnley & Pendle Transport 121 (KBB 521L) is seen at Burnley bus station on 21 July 1984. An early Leyland National new to Tyne & Wear Passenger Transport Executive in 1972, she was 11.3 metres long and had a dual-doorway layout with forty-four seats.

Arriving at Showbus, Duxford, in 1999 is preserved London Transport OJD 903R, which was delivered new as LS103 in June 1977. Sold via PVS Carlton to Port of Ramsgate in 1990, she entered preservation in 1999 and was last recorded in 2015 as being with the Scottish Vintage Bus Museum in Lathalmond.

Blackpool Borough Transport 546 (CFM 347S) is seen in Blackpool town centre on 18 August 1986. She was new as Crosville SNL347 in 1978, and was 11.3 metres long with forty-nine seats. Crosville replaced the Leyland 510 engine with a Gardner 6HLX engine. After Blackpool, CFM 347S saw further service with W. Norfolk & Sons of Nayland in Suffolk.

Sovereign Bus & Coach FUG 323T started life with West Yorkshire when she was purchased new by that company in March 1979. In this view of St Albans City station on 28 May 1992, she is working local service S2 between New Greens and Mile House.

LMA 413T was new to Crosville in 1979 as fleet number SNL413. Later fitted with a Gardner 6HLX engine by Crosville, she became SNG413. In 1986 Blackpool Borough Transport bought four Gardner-engined Leyland Nationals from Crosville, one of which was LMA 413T. In 1990 W. Norfolk & Sons of Nayland bought these four Leyland Nationals and on 9 March 1991 LMA 413T is seen with Norfolk's at Colchester bus station.

Making the journey in 1996 from Walthamstow in East London out to Basildon in Essex is Thamesway's WJN 565S. She was new to Eastern National in January 1978.

In 1984 Blackpool Borough Transport bought four Leyland National 2, each of which were 11.6 metres long, had forty-nine seats and were powered by Gardner 6HLXCT engines. Here, 544 (A544 PCW) is seen in Blackpool town centre on 18 August 1986. A nice touch of municipal pride was the Blackpool coat of arms above the Leyland name on the front grille.

Like neighbouring Eastern National, London Country took a large number of Leyland Nationals, bypassing the Bristol RE completely. New in March 1976, and by now carrying Townlink fleet names, LPB 227P arrives at Waltham Cross in 1991.

Ribble 758 (UHG 758R) was new in 1977, and was 11.3 metres long with forty-nine seats. She is seen in Wigan on 18 August 1986 in standard National Bus Company livery, including the white band.

New to United Auto in January 1982, Leyland National RDC 734X was part of the Tees fleet when photographed in Stockton-on-Tees in May 1991.

The Leyland National 2 had the option of a full heating and ventilating system with the pod on the rear roof, or a conventional heating system which did not require the pod. The latter option is shown by Ribble 866 (LFR 866X) in Wigan on 2 June 1984. She was new in 1982, and was 10.6 metres long with forty-four seats and a Leyland engine.

The Bee Line's NRD 134M was a Leyland National with B49F bodywork that was new to Alder Valley in August 1973. Some twenty years later she was captured passing through Slough on 22 May 1993.

Stagecoach Ribble Bus 301 (CHH 214T) is seen in Clitheroe on 5 July 1995. She was new to Cumberland Motor Services in 1979 and was a series B model, being 10.3 metres long with forty-four seats. By this time, both Ribble and Cumberland had become part of the Stagecoach Group.

The town centre in Woodbridge was certainly not designed for large vehicles. Making the right turn from the town centre at Cross Corner in 1981 is Eastern Counties LN599 (WVF 599S). Many drivers preferred to go straight ahead at this junction and go 'around the block' to approach in a straight line, thus avoiding the risk of the rear overhang hitting the building.

Long-established independent operator John Fishwick & Sons of Leyland had a history of buying Leyland buses, being as they were based near the Leyland factory. Fishwick's bought Leyland Nationals as well, even though they were built at Workington in Cumbria. Seen at Fishwick's depot in Golden Hill Lane, Leyland, on 18 August 1994 are Leyland National 2 16 (OFV 620X), which was new in 1981, and an earlier Leyland National, 1 (NFR 558T), which was new in 1979.

New to Ribble in November 1981 was this Leyland National, LFR 860X, which is seen at Showbus, Woburn, on 27 September 1992 as part of the Cumberland fleet, wearing Stagecoach stripes livery.

Yorkshire Traction 244 (NKU 244X), new in 1981, was an 11.6-metre-long Leyland National 2 with a Leyland engine and fifty-two seats. She is seen leaving Doncaster bus station for Barnsley on 25 April 1991. In the background is another Yorkshire Traction Leyland National 2, 233 (LWE 233W), which is seen working a local service.

New to Provincial in May 1984 was A301 KJT, seen arriving at Showbus, Duxford, in 1999.

Wilfreda Beehive operate British and European coach holidays. In the years after bus deregulation they operated local bus services in Doncaster as well, where 70 (HHY 816N) was spotted on 25 April 1991. She was new to Bristol Omnibus Company in 1975 as fleet number C1455, the C denoting allocation to Bristol city services. HHY 816N was 11.3 metres long with forty-four seats and a dual-doorway layout.

Sovereign Leyland National DPH 503T passes through Watford on 11 March 1993. This bus had been new to London Country with B41F bodywork in August 1979.

With privatisation, the livery of West Yorkshire Road Car Company changed from National Bus Company poppy red and white back to Tilling red and cream. Unfortunately, in the years after privatisation the company was split up and sold off to different owners. 1529 (UWY 71X), seen in York on 18 November 1989, carries the Tilling red and cream livery, but with Harrogate & District fleet names. Harrogate & District became part of the Blazefield Group, now the Transdev Group. 1529 was new in 1981, and was 11.6 metres long with a Leyland engine and fifty-two seats.

New in December 1977 to Eastern National, Leyland National VAR 898S was still working for the company when photographed in the bus station in Colchester in 1996.

Keighley & District was another part of the West Yorkshire Road Car Company that became part of the Blazefield, now Transdev Group. In Keighley on 13 June 1991 was 271 (PWY 583W), which was new to West Yorkshire Road Car in 1980. This Leyland National 2 was 10.6 metres long with a Leyland engine and forty-four seats.

South Riding's CUP 659S was new to United in February 1978. She is seen here in Sheffield on 12 September 1992.

The West Yorkshire Road Car operations in York became Rider (York) as part of Yorkshire Rider, which was bought by Badgerline Holdings. Leyland National 2 1353 (UWY 75X) was photographed opposite York railway station on 19 January 1991, with the city walls in the background. 11.6 metres long with a Leyland engine and fifty-two seats, she was new to West Yorkshire Road Car in 1981.

Leyland National YAZ 4143 was part of the Kimes of Folkingham fleet, and is seen at Showbus, Duxford, in 1999.

First Calderline 1367 (MHJ 723V) is seen leaving Halifax bus station on 12 February 1999. This Leyland National 2 was new to Eastern National in 1980 with fleet number 1927 and was transferred to Yorkshire Rider in 1994. At that time, both companies were in the Badgerline Group. Later under First Group ownership, Yorkshire Rider was split into separate operating companies with their own liveries, as seen here.

New to the Bristol Omnibus Company in July 1980, AAE 655V moved within First Group to Eastern Counties, and she is seen here in the Grange Farm area of Felixstowe on a wet Sunday in 1999.

British Leyland worked with its Leyland DAB subsidiary in Denmark to develop articulated buses for the South Yorkshire Passenger Transport Executive. They used a Leyland DAB mid-engined chassis with a Leyland TL11 engine and a Leyland National 2 body. There were three doors and sixty seats. One of the South Yorkshire PTE buses, 2008 (FHE 291V), was trialled in passenger service by Ipswich Borough Transport in November 1981 on service 13 to the Chantry Estate, and is seen here negotiating the St Matthews Street roundabout in Ipswich.

It is 8.10 a.m. on Tuesday 27 February 2018 at Market Lane, Terrington St Clement, and about to start the school run from Walpole St Andrew to Marshland High School, West Walton, is UFX 852S. School children just do not realise how lucky they are to travel to school on such a wonderful vehicle. Lucky kids! (Photograph: Julian Patterson).

Eastern National's YEV 323S enters the bus station in Colchester in 1996, having been new to this operator in May 1978.

Their working lives over, a pair of withdrawn Eastern Counties Leyland Nationals stand at Ipswich in 1991.

About the Authors

Robert Appleton

I was born on 15 April 1954 and I grew up in the village of Mistley, near Manningtree, Essex. I passed the 11 plus exam and went to Colchester Royal Grammar School. After A levels, I went to work for Norwich Union Insurance in Ipswich in 1972.

My career with Norwich Union, which later became Aviva, took me to Watford and Manchester. I married in 1998. I worked for Norwich Union/Aviva for forty years and retired in 2012. By then my wife's parents had died and we took the decision to move back to north-east Essex to look after my mother, who still lives in Mistley.

My interest in buses started with travelling from Mistley to school in Colchester on the buses of the Eastern Counties Omnibus Company Ltd.

My late father was a keen amateur photographer and he encouraged my interest in photography. In 1969 he obtained a second-hand Exacta 35 mm camera for me, which gave much better results than my first camera, so I was able to combine photography with my enthusiasm for buses in East Anglia, and beyond.

Robert Appleton
26 February 2018

Peter Horrex

I grew up in Kesgrave on the outskirts of Ipswich in Suffolk during the 1960s and 1970s, becoming interested in buses in 1976 after my first ride on a Bristol Lodekka.

After leaving school in 1978 I worked for G. E. Woodward, a local family office equipment company based in Princes Street, Ipswich, and from there I made the decision in 1986 to move to London to work as a bus driver, passing through London Transport's Chiswick training school later that same year. I've driven many types of bus in service, not just in London, but also when I worked as a bus driver in Stevenage and with First Eastern Counties in Ipswich.

I've been back in London now for the past eleven years, driving buses in the Enfield area, but the enthusiast in me still misses the wonderful era of the seventies and eighties, of the National Bus Company and the buses of that time.

Peter Horrex
26 February 2018

Bibliography

Books

Eastern National and Thamesway Fleet Record: Vol. 2 (Essex Bus Enthusiasts Group).
Fleet History of Colchester Corporation and Successors (PSV Circle).
London Independents Fleet Book (British Bus Publishing).
North West Fleet Book (British Bus Publishing).
Yorkshire Bus Fleet Book (British Bus Publishing).

Websites

Bus Lists on the Web (www.buslistsontheweb.co.uk).
Ian's Bus Stop (www.countrybus.org).